FRANCE
the culture

Greg Nickles

A Bobbie Kalman Book

The Lands, Peoples, and Cultures Series

 Crabtree Publishing Company

The Lands, Peoples, and Cultures Series
Created by Bobbie Kalman

Coordinating editor
Ellen Rodger

Project development, editing, and photo research
First Folio Resource Group, Inc.
Pauline Beggs
Tom Dart
Kathryn Lane
Debbie Smith

Design
David Vereschagin/Quadrat Communications

Separations and film
Embassy Graphics

Printer
Worzalla Publishing Company

Consultant
Thérèse Sabaryn, University of Waterloo;
Daphnée Saurel

Photographs
George Ancona/International Stock Photo: p. 7 (middle); AP/Wide World Photos: p. 25 (bottom); Archiv/Photo Researchers: p. 25 (top), p. 28 (top), p. 29 (left); Archive Photos: p. 24 (both); Belzaux/Rapho/Photo Researchers: p. 15 (top); Christophe Bluntzer/Impact: title page; Thierry Bouzac/Impact: p. 5 (bottom right); Dale E. Boyer/Photo Researchers: p. 4 (bottom); Van Bucher/Photo Researchers: p. 17 (top); William Carter/Photo Researchers: p. 13 (top); Corbis/Dave Bartruff: p. 8 (left); Corbis/Bettmann: p. 28 (bottom); Corbis/Leonard de Selva: p. 22 (bottom); Corbis/Michelle Garrett: p. 8 (right); Corbis/Chris Hellier: p. 21 (bottom); Corbis/Robert Holmes: p. 27 (bottom); Corbis/Charles and Josette Lenars: p. 10 (bottom); Corbis/José F. Poblete: p. 11 (top); Corbis/The Purcell Team: p. 18; Corbis/Manfred Vollmer: p. 11 (bottom); Corbis/Inge Yspeert: p. 29 (right); Walter Daran/Archive Photos: p. 4 (top); François Ducasse/Rapho/Photo Researchers: p. 14 (top); Richard Frieman/Photo Researchers: p. 23 (right); Gordon Gahan/Photo Researchers: p. 22 (top); Giraudon/Art Resource, NY: p. 5 (top right), p. 12 (top), p. 14 (bottom); Sylvain Grandadam/Photo Researchers: p. 5 (left); George Haling/Photo Researchers: p. 19 (top right); Mike J. Howell/International Stock Photo: p. 19 (bottom); Wolfgang Kaehler: p. 21 (top); Kammerman/Rapho/Photo Researchers: p. 12 (bottom); Alain Le Garsmeur/Impact: contents page; Erich Lessing/Art Resource, NY: p. 16 (both), p. 23 (left); Philip Mould/Bridgeman Art Library: p. 27 (top); Richard T. Nowitz: p. 26; A. Philippon/Explorer: p. 9 (both); Christine Porter/Impact: p. 10 (top); Porterfield/Chickering/Photo Researchers: cover; Science Photo Library/Photo Researchers: p. 25 (middle); Roger Markham Smith/International Stock Photo: p. 7 (top); Stockman/International Stock Photo: p. 19 (top left); Tate Gallery, London/Art Resource, NY: p. 17 (bottom); Catherine Ursillo/Photo Researchers: p. 15 (bottom), p. 20 (bottom); Theodore Vogel/Impact: p. 7 (bottom); Sabine Weiss/Photo Researchers: p. 6; Sabine Weiss/Rapho/Photo Researchers: p. 13 (bottom); Hilary Wilkes/International Stock Photo: p. 20 (top)

Illustrations
Alexei Mezentsev: pp. 30–31
David Wysotski, Allure Illustrations: back cover

Cover: Beautiful gardens stand in front of the Château de Villandry, a castle in the Loire Valley.

Title page: The Arc de Triomphe du Carrousel in front of the Louvre museum in Paris was built by Napoleon in 1805, to celebrate his military victories.

Icon: The Notre Dame cathedral appears at the head of each spread.

Back cover: Gothic cathedrals such as Notre Dame are decorated with grotesque ornamental figures called gargoyles.

Published by
Crabtree Publishing Company

PMB 16A
350 Fifth Avenue
Suite 3308
New York
N.Y. 10118

612 Welland Avenue
St. Catharines
Ontario, Canada
L2M 5V6

73 Lime Walk
Headington
Oxford OX3 7AD
United Kingdom

Cataloging in Publication Data
Nickles, Greg, 1969-
   France, the culture / Greg Nickles.
      p.cm -- (The lands, peoples, and cultures series)
   "A Bobbie Kalman book."
   Includes index.
      Summary: A survey of modern and ancient France, focusing on language, religion, art, festivals, fashion and architecture.
      ISBN 0-86505-323-5 (paper) -- ISBN 0-86505-243-3 (rlb.)
      1. France--Civilization--Juvenile literature. 2. France--Social life and customs--Juvenile literature. I. Title.II Series.
   DC33.N52 2000
   j944   LC00-025730
                                         CIP

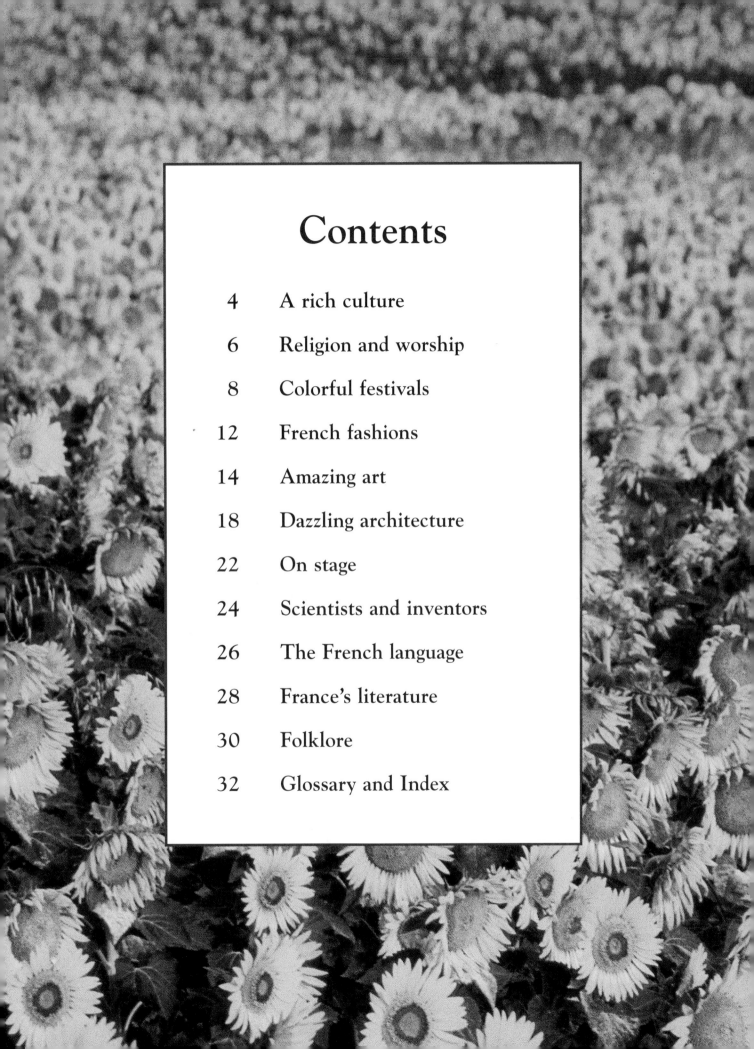

Contents

France's rich culture stretches back many centuries. For much of this time, French artists created works for churches, kings, and **aristocrats**. Architects built beautiful buildings with stunning gardens and fountains. People all over the country developed and celebrated their own **customs**, folk arts, and ways of dress.

(right) Edith Piaf (1915–1963) was one of France's most loved singers. She sang sad songs about the hardships of life.

(below) Cherubs adorn the Pont Alexandre III, the most elaborate bridge crossing the Seine River in Paris.

Ideas that changed the world

For the last 300 years, France's culture has influenced the culture of many countries in Europe and North America. Since the eighteenth century, France has been home to artists who have created **controversial** new forms of painting, sculpture, music, and dance. **Revolutionary** French thinkers have become leaders in **philosophy**, fashion, literature, and science. Their ideas have changed history. Today, they continue to challenge and inspire people all over the world.

(above) Henri de Toulouse-Lautrec (1864–1901) painted scenes of Paris night life. He created this poster advertising the famous nightclub, the Moulin Rouge, in 1891.

(above) An organ grinder plays music for passers-by while his cat and dog sleep soundly.

(right) An artist daubs make-up on a model's face before a street performance.

The Saint Jean de Luz church, in Biarritz, is packed for the Sunday service.

Many French people belong to the Roman Catholic or Protestant Church. Both these churches are **denominations** of Christianity, the religion based on the teachings of Jesus Christ. Other main religions in France are Islam and Judaism. Islam's teachings are found in the holy book called the Qur'an, while Judaism's teachings are written in the Torah.

Christianity

Christianity is about 2000 years old. It is based on the worship of Jesus Christ, whose teachings were recorded in the Bible. Christians believe that Jesus was the son of God. They also believe that he performed miracles, such as curing people's illnesses and returning to life after he was crucified, or put to death on a cross. Christ's mother, Mary, and other holy people, called saints, are also important in Christianity.

Christians in France

Within a few centuries, Christianity spread through Europe, including France. Gradually, the Roman Catholic Church became a major part of France's arts, festivals, and everyday life.

Throughout Europe in the 1500s, a group of Christians called Protestants broke away from the Roman Catholic Church and formed their own church. Bloody wars broke out between the two groups. Many French Protestants, called Huguenots, were murdered or forced to leave France.

The Roman Catholic Church remained powerful until the French **Revolution** in 1789. Then, the king, who supported the Roman Catholic Church, was forced to step down. France's new government refused to keep Christianity as the country's official religion.

Roman Catholic ceremonies

Today, most people in France are Roman Catholics, though there are about a million Protestants. On the whole, however, few French Christians **worship** regularly. Most Roman Catholics in France attend church only for major religious holidays or important events. One of the most important events is a baptism. Most people are baptized when they are babies. The **priest** sprinkles holy water on the person's head, welcoming him or her into the Church and washing away sin. At age eleven or twelve, boys and girls become full members of the Church after their confirmation. During the confirmation ceremony, children state that they understand the rules of their religion.

(above) During Roman Catholic services, people take communion, the tasting of holy bread or the host. At the age of seven or eight, children dress in white for their first communion.

The Miracle of Lourdes

Lourdes, in southwest France, is one of the holiest sites in Europe. It became famous in 1858 when Bernadette Soubirous, a local girl, claimed that Jesus' mother, Mary, miraculously appeared before her in a cave eighteen times. Mary guided Bernadette to a spot on the ground. When Bernadette scratched at the spot, a spring of water gushed out. Since then, masses of people regularly visit Lourdes to light candles, pray, and try the spring water which is believed to cure illnesses.

(above) Jewish men carefully unroll a Torah scroll, which is written in Hebrew.

(left) A Muslim boy follows the teachings of Islam and studies Arabic, the language in which the Qur'an is written.

7

The French calendar is filled with *fêtes,* or festivals. These *fêtes* are celebrated with tasty food, colorful decorations, loud music, and exciting games. Some *fêtes* are traditional religious holidays. Others mark the anniversary of historical events. Still others are annual **agricultural**, sporting, or arts festivals.

Noël

Noël, or Christmas, falls on December 25. This holiday marks the birth of Jesus Christ. It is celebrated with a special season of events. On the eve of *Noël*, family members gather for a special feast. Later that evening, many families go to church for a special service called midnight mass. At the church, people often perform traditional plays that re-enact the nativity, or Christ's birth. Before going to bed that night, children leave out their shoes, hoping that *Père Noël*, the French Santa Claus, will place small gifts inside. They also leave *Père Noël* a cup of hot chocolate or cocoa.

Children gather around Père Noël during a Christmas parade.

Other *Noël* customs include decorating Christmas trees and keeping a *crèche*. A *crèche* is a special crib in which people place nativity figures, or *santons.* The Christmas season ends on January 6, which is called the Epiphany. People celebrate the Epiphany by eating a special cake called *la galette des rois,* or "the cake of kings." Whoever finds a bean or plastic figure in their piece of cake wins the title of king or queen for the day.

La Chandeleur

Christians celebrate *La Chandeleur,* or Candlemas, on February 2. This festival remembers the day when Mary first presented Jesus at the **temple**. On *La Chandeleur,* a priest blesses worshipers' candles. People also eat *crêpes*, or thin pancakes, which they believe will ensure a good **harvest**. A favorite tradition while preparing *crêpes* is to hold a coin in one hand and a *crêpe* pan in the other. It is said that whoever can flip their *crêpe* with one hand without dropping it will be wealthy and healthy for the year.

*A cook has flipped many **crêpes** in preparation for the feast of **La Chandeleur.***

Mardi Gras

In February, the city of Nice holds the twelve-day *Mardi Gras* Carnival, one of the largest festivals in the country. *"Mardi Gras"* means "Fat Tuesday" or "Shrove Tuesday." It refers to the last day that people can eat rich foods before the beginning of Lent, which is traditionally a six-week period of **fasting**.

Long live the king!

Mardi Gras festivities begin with an evening parade for the **mascot**, King Carnival. King Carnival is a large effigy, or stuffed figure. The next day is the *Grand Corso,* or "Big Parade." It features brightly colored floats accompanied by costumed riders on elegant white horses. Bands in uniform march alongside, playing all types of music. They are joined by hundreds of people wearing huge, comical *papier mâché* heads that resemble animals, food, or famous people.

The Battle of Flowers

Shrove Tuesday, the carnival's last day, begins with the Battle of Flowers. During this battle, people riding horse-drawn carriages harmlessly throw all colors and kinds of flowers at onlookers. Spectators are welcome to bring their own flowers and fight back! Then, people parade the effigy of King Carnival to the seaside and burn it. Brilliant fireworks follow, and the day ends with a grand masked ball.

Around Easter

People throughout the country mark Shrove Tuesday by eating *crêpes.* The following day, Lent begins. Six weeks later, Christians celebrate *Pâques,* or Easter. During *Pâques,* special church services, music, and parades honor Jesus Christ's death and return to life. At home, many children celebrate the holiday by receiving chocolate chickens and going on Easter egg hunts.

*(left) The queen of the **Mardi Gras Carnival** is ready for the Battle of Flowers.*

*(below) Thousands of people line the streets of Nice during the **Mardi Gras** parade, watching the floats go by.*

A bakery displays a special fish-shaped loaf of bread for **Poisson d'avril.**

April Fool's!

On the first day of April, many people in France celebrate *Poisson d'avril,* or April Fool's Day. *Poisson d'avril* is a day of tricks, jokes, and fun gifts. A favorite prank is to secretly stick a small cloth or paper *poisson,* or fish, on someone's back. When a person is caught with the fish on his or her back, people point and say, *"Poisson d'avril!"*

Bastille Day

Bastille Day, on July 14, is France's national holiday. It honors the day in 1789 when 600 Parisians stormed the king's Bastille prison and started the French Revolution. Throughout the country, people celebrate Bastille Day with parades, street fairs, live music, dancing, and fireworks. Paris, France's **capital**, holds the largest celebrations. Hundreds of thousands of people line the *Champs Élysées,* one of Paris's main streets, to watch the nation's official **military** parade. Marching bands play the national anthem, *"La Marseillaise."* Later, bonfires and brilliant fireworks light up the night sky.

Local *fêtes*

Besides their large *fêtes,* the French hold hundreds of local celebrations. Cities often host large arts festivals, while towns and villages celebrate events such as the harvest or the bottling of a new batch of wines.

Film at Cannes

In the late 1800s, the French made the first motion pictures. Today, movies are still important in the country. Each May, the southern city of Cannes hosts the world's most respected film festival. Movie stars, directors, and other filmmakers present their latest work and compete for the festival's top prizes. Thousands of fans also come to watch films or catch a glimpse of famous people.

Jets stream red, white, and blue trails, the colors of the French flag, over Bastille Day festivities in Paris.

Men carry a statue of a saint, or holy person, out of a church during a **pardon**. *Other people will join the procession and carry banners through the streets.*

Pardons in Brittany

Throughout Brittany, a region in northwest France, villages hold annual religious events called *pardons*. At the *pardons*, people pray to be forgiven for their wrongdoings and to be cured of illnesses. The villagers, many in traditional costume, gather at the church for a service. After a parade through town, they spend the day visiting neighbors.

The Festival of Cornouaille

Each July, people in the town of Quimper, in Brittany, host a seven-day festival to celebrate the traditions of their **ancestors**, the Celts. The Celts arrived from central Europe around 1000 B.C. The Festival of Cornouaille, named after the area around Quimper, includes hundreds of traditional events, from dances to wrestling matches and parades. Storytellers and puppet shows retell old Celtic tales, while craftspeople show off their wares. Huge meals, featuring *crêpes* and seafood, are also part of the fun.

Musicians playing bagpipes, traditional Celtic instruments, march in a Festival of Cornouaille parade.

11

Since the fourteenth century, the French have been known for their stylish clothing. Today, Paris is the center of the international fashion industry and the home of many famous designers. Many people in France dress in these designers' elegant or casual clothing. Each region in France also has unique traditional costumes that people wear on special occasions.

High fashion

For hundreds of years, France's rulers and aristocrats set the trends for elegant dress among the leaders of Europe. Their extremely expensive costumes, made by personal tailors, often included large wigs, fine silks, and **embroidered** coats. Then, in Paris during the 1800s, the first fashion houses began to set the styles. Today, these companies still lead the world in creating exciting new clothes, which are shown off in flashy fashion shows.

(above) In this painting by Louise Elizabeth Vigee-Lebrun, the French queen Marie Antoinette wears an outfit typical of the French nobility in the late 1700s.

(right) Coco Chanel (1883–1971) was one of the most influential fashion designers ever. She created simple, sophisticated styles for women.

Regional clothing

Many unique costumes in each region of France were once everyday garments. Today, they are usually worn only by older people or by those dressing up for festivals. The distinctive black **beret**, however, is a common sight all over France.

Breton fashion

The traditional costumes of Brittany are some of the best known in the country. At festivals, weddings, and other special occasions, Breton men commonly wear a broad, black hat and white shirt with a dark vest and baggy pants. Women wear long dresses, often made of black velvet or satin, with collars of white lace. One of the most interesting parts of a Breton woman's costume is her headdress. These special hats are made of white lace or linen. They vary in size and shape throughout Brittany.

Teenagers in traditional costume chat during a festival in Brittany.

Girls wearing traditional Basque costumes dance outside. The Basque people live in the southwest area of France and in northern Spain.

France has been home to some of the world's greatest artists. Many have been French, but some came from other countries, attracted by France's reputation as a center for the arts. Their works are displayed in galleries and museums across France. The largest is the Louvre museum in Paris, which houses about 30,000 pieces of art.

Lascaux caves

The cave paintings near the town of Lascaux, in southwest France, are some of the world's oldest pieces of artwork. They remained hidden until four teenagers discovered them by accident in 1940. As people began to visit the Lascaux caves, air from the outside damaged the paintings. The caves were closed to the public in 1963. Today, exact copies of the paintings, created with the same techniques and materials as the original artists used, are on display at a nearby site called Lascaux II.

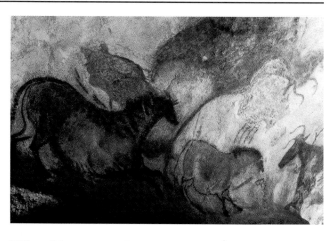

(top right) The paintings of bulls, horses, and bison in the Lascaux caves date back 15,000 to 20,000 years!

(below) French troops stand ready to attack the English in a section of the Bayeux Tapestry.

The Bayeux Tapestry

About a thousand years ago, art in France usually portrayed kings, aristocrats, or religious subjects. The Bayeux **Tapestry**, woven on a 70-meter (230-foot) long piece of **linen**, is a treasure from this time. **Nuns** in Bayeux, a town along France's northern coast, made it over a period of ten years. The tapestry is decorated with more than 50 scenes that show how William the Conqueror, a local duke, **invaded** England and became its new king. Surrounding the tapestry is a border with pictures of beasts from fables and other ancient stories.

Jacques-Louis David (1748–1825) became the court painter for Napoleon I. In this painting, Napoleon crowns himself emperor and makes his wife Josephine the empress.

Styles of their own

For hundreds of years, France's painters and sculptors followed artistic styles that were popular in other countries. It was not until the 1700s that French painters began to lead the world with their own styles. One of France's most famous early masters was Jacques-Louis David. David painted heroic, lifelike portraits of French leaders and scenes from the ancient Greek and Roman **civilizations**. Later painters portrayed everyday subjects in their work. Gustav Courbet, for example, painted ordinary people in a style that was called Realism.

*In the 1860s, Auguste Rodin's sculptures looked unfinished to many people. He is now considered one of the greatest sculptors of all time, and **The Thinker** is one of the most famous sculptures in the world.*

In paintings such as **Le Moulin de la Galette** *(1876), the Impressionist painter Pierre Auguste Renoir captured the friendliness and fun of the outdoor café scene in Paris.*

Impressionism

In the last half of the nineteenth century, French artists continued to invent new ways of painting. One group of artists, known as the Impressionists, were not interested in creating lifelike pictures. Instead, they created an impression of a scene, using quick dabs and strokes of color to capture their subject in the changing sunlight.

Post-Impressionism

The bold, colorful paintings of the Impressionists inspired many new artists to experiment with their own styles. The French artist Paul Gauguin used strong colors and shapes to express emotion. Vincent Van Gogh, who was originally from Holland, lived in France while he painted his famous canvases using swirling, thick strokes of bright colors.

Claude Monet (1840–1926), another Impressionist artist, made 40 paintings of the cathedral in Rouen, each under different lighting conditions. Here, he painted the cathedral through dense, gray fog.

The post-Impressionist Georges Seurat created paintings, such as **Sunday Afternoon on the Island,** *made up of thousands of points of color.*

Modern art

By the beginning of the twentieth century, artists in France were abandoning all traditions and inventing new, "modern" art. Henri Matisse and a group of painters called the *Fauves,* or "wild beasts," used fantastic colors to paint their subjects. The **rebellious** Marcel Duchamp made ordinary objects into art simply by autographing them. By World War II, people were creating modern art in any shape or form.

Georges Braque was a Cubist. His wildly geometric paintings, such as **Bottles and Fish,** *showed many different sides of a subject at once.*

Notre Dame is an excellent example of gothic architecture. Two bell towers, each with 387 steps, rise at the front (left); flying buttresses support the walls at the back (right); and the round stained-glass South Rose Window measures 13 meters (43 feet) across.

There are magnificent buildings of all ages and styles throughout France. Everything from ancient ruins and old **cathedrals** to ultra-modern offices and apartments stand in the cities and countryside.

Houses of worship

Some of France's most impressive buildings are its cathedrals. They were built centuries ago as places of Christian worship. The cathedrals are richly decorated with stained glass, wall paintings, and stone carvings that show religious scenes. Each building took thousands of workers decades and sometimes even centuries to complete. Many people worked their entire life on just one cathedral!

Notre Dame and Chartres

Two of France's best known cathedrals are Notre Dame, in the heart of Paris, and Chartres, southwest of Paris. Notre Dame took 200 years to build and was completed in the 1300s. Its stone walls are decorated with rows of statues and gargoyles, which are strange, imaginary creatures. The building of Chartres Cathedral began in 1020, but around 1200 it was almost completely destroyed in a fire. The cathedral was rebuilt in an impressively short 25 years, complete with 3000 square meters (32,300 square feet) of stained-glass windows.

Stained-glass windows adorn cathedrals all over France. Some, like this window, are relatively new. Others have remained unbroken for almost a thousand years.

The Pont du Gard aqueduct was built by the Romans, who invaded France about 2000 years ago. Water ran along a channel at the top of the bridge, transporting it over the Gardon River during its route from fresh-water springs to the Roman settlement of Nîmes.

Mont-Saint-Michel

Mont-Saint-Michel, off France's northern coast, is one of the country's major attractions. Over a thousand years ago, Christian **monks** built an **abbey** on top of the rocky island, where they could live a life devoted to prayer. Over the years, **fortified** walls and a small village were added to Mont-Saint-Michel. The island is completely surrounded by water when the tides are very high. At other times, soft sand surrounds Mont-Saint-Michel. A causeway, or raised road built across the sand and water, allows people to reach Mont-Saint-Michel.

For 73 years following the French Revolution, Mont-Saint-Michel was a jail for political prisoners.

(above) King Francis I built one of France's most beautiful **châteaux**, *Chambord, in 1519. This huge mansion has 440 rooms and 84 staircases!*

Palaces and *châteaux*

Many of France's most splendid palaces and *châteaux*, or country mansions, were built centuries ago in the Loire Valley. Some were built as fortified castles to defend against attack. Others were built as holiday retreats. Their owners filled the large rooms with luxurious furnishings, tapestries, and other rich decorations. Today, France's greatest palaces are museums. Some *châteaux* are still owned by wealthy families, while others are used as inns or rented out for special events.

The palace of Versailles

The palace of Versailles was built in the 1600s. For a hundred years, during the time of Kings Louis XIII, XIV, and XV, it was the center of power in France and the scene of lavish parties and banquets. It took about 40,000 workers to build the huge complex of buildings and gardens at Versailles. Once completed, Versailles housed thousands of people, including aristocrats, servants, politicians, and the king and queen.

In the lap of luxury

The hundreds of rooms in the palace of Versailles include luxurious apartments, a **chapel**, an opera house, and the throne room. These rooms are decorated with ceiling **murals**, colored marble, golden carvings, and even a clock that is supposed to keep time until the year 9999! The palace is surrounded by vast gardens with beautiful fountains, including one in the shape of a dragon. There is also a 1.6-kilometer (1-mile) long Grand Canal, where royal boating parties were once held.

One of the most spectacular rooms at Versailles is the 72-meter (236-foot) long Hall of Mirrors, in which seventeen huge mirrors hang on the walls.

Modern architecture

France is also famous for its many modern buildings, including remarkable apartment projects and office complexes. *La Défense*, in Paris, is the largest business center in Europe. Its space-age buildings include *La Grande Arche*, an office tower that looks like a hollow cube. The colorful Pompidou Center, a center for the arts in Paris, has its pipes, ducts, escalators, and **girders**, which are normally inside a building, on the outside.

The brightly painted pipes and ducts of the Pompidou Center are color coded: elevators are red, air ducts blue, electrical lines yellow, and water pipes green.

Cheval's *Palais Idéal*

The *Palais Idéal* is in the small village of Hauterives in southeast France. This fantasy palace was constructed single-handedly by Ferdinand Cheval, a postman, beginning in the late 1800s. The structure is made out of the stones that Cheval collected while he was delivering mail. Although his neighbors thought he was crazy, many artists in the early 1900s admired Cheval's imitation of Egyptian, **Aztec**, and Asian designs.

Ferdinand Cheval worked long and hard to make his dream come true. Inside his palace is an inscription: "1879–1912: 10,000 days, 93,000 hours, 33 years of toil."

A young girl enjoys an outdoor minstrel puppet show in a Paris park.

On any day in France, it is easy to find exciting concerts, dance performances, puppet shows, and pantomime acts. Paris is the busiest spot, but many music, dance, and theater events are held throughout the country.

Making music

Centuries ago, music was either religious and performed in churches, or it was played for aristocrats by traveling minstrels. The minstrels were musicians who also juggled and did acrobatics. In the 1800s, the music scene changed when French **composers** began creating great symphonies and operas.

LA DAMNATION DE FAUST, PAR M. HECTOR BERLIOZ.

Composers in France

Hector Berlioz was one of the greatest French composers of the 1800s and is considered the father of the modern orchestra. His sweeping, emotional music, including *Fantastic Symphony,* required orchestras to play a greater number of instruments than they had ever played before. Claude Debussy composed music inspired by Impressionist paintings. His pieces, including *Prelude to the Afternoon of a Faun,* used soft, wandering melodies to create dreamlike moods. Other composers include piano master Frederic Chopin, originally from Poland, and Georges Bizet, who composed the popular opera *Carmen.* Today, Pierre Boulez's experimental, often tuneless music is regarded as some of the most important in France.

In 1846, Hector Berlioz composed **The Damnation of Faust** *for a choir and orchestra. The piece tells the story of Faust, a scholar who sold his soul to the devil in exchange for knowledge, eternal youth, and magical powers.*

Puppetry

Both children and adults enjoy summertime outdoor puppet shows. Some puppets are hand puppets, like the traditional character of Polichinelle. Other puppets are marionettes, which are operated from above by as many as 30 strings.

Pantomime artists tell stories using facial expressions and body movement, rather than words. Marcel Marceau popularized the ancient art of mime with his character, Bip.

The energetic cancan, in which a line of women wearing ruffled skirts kick so high that their slips show, became popular and controversial during the 1800s. A few men have joined the cancan line in this painting by Georges Seurat, called Le Chahut, *which means* The Uproar.

Dance in France

France's most popular dance, ballet, was imported from Italy in the late 1500s. At first, it was a simple mix of music, pantomime, and drama that was performed by aristocrats. In the 1600s, however, King Louis XIV established the first professional ballet school. In the years that followed, the French pioneered the graceful leaps and spins that we recognize today. Two favorite ballets, *La Sylphide* and *Giselle,* were created in France in the nineteenth century. Both tell the sad story of lost love.

More recently, Roland Petit, a French dancer and choreographer, brought new life to ballet in France after World War II. He created more than 50 ballets with beautiful sets and costumes for the world's best-known dancers.

23

Scientists and inventors

Over the last four centuries, the French have made scientific discoveries and created inventions that have changed the world. Today, they continue to be world leaders in the fields of medicine, chemistry, ocean research, and space flight.

Louis Pasteur

Louis Pasteur was one of the greatest medical researchers of the nineteenth century. His discovery that bacteria, or germs, spread disease helped doctors develop ways to cure and prevent illness. Pasteur himself invented a **vaccine** and cure for rabies, a disease that had been deadly until his discovery.

Marie and Pierre Curie

In the early 1900s, Marie Curie, who was originally from Poland, and her husband, Pierre, made important advances in the new field of nuclear physics, or the study of atoms. Their discoveries later led to the invention of **nuclear power** and helped doctors find treatments for diseases such as cancer. They shared the Nobel prize for physics in 1903 and Marie won the Nobel prize for chemistry in 1911, after Pierre's death. Marie Curie was the first woman to receive a Nobel prize in chemistry and the first person ever to receive two Nobel prizes in science.

Louis Pasteur invented pasteurization, a technique that helps to preserve milk by killing the bacteria that makes it sour quickly.

The Curies work in their lab. The materials that Marie Curie was exposed to through her research eventually led to her death.

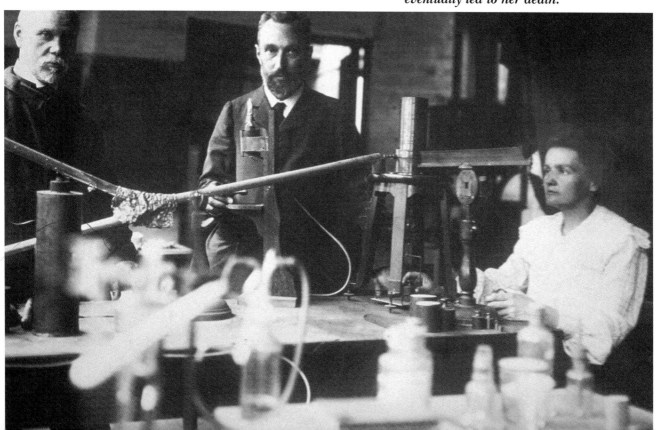

In this drawing, Joseph and Étienne Montgolfier give a public demonstration of their invention, the hot air balloon, in 1783.

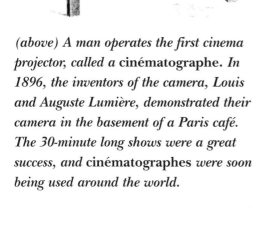

Jacques Cousteau

Jacques Cousteau was the twentieth century's leading oceanographer, or ocean scientist. With Émile Gagnan, he invented the aqualung, a portable breathing system that allows divers to swim deep underwater without being tied to an air line from the surface. For decades, Cousteau traveled the world aboard his ship, the *Calypso*, documenting new discoveries and encouraging people to save plants and animals in nature.

(below) Jacques Cousteau prepares for a dive in 1974, to search for the lost island of Atlantis.

(above) A man operates the first cinema projector, called a **cinématographe.** *In 1896, the inventors of the camera, Louis and Auguste Lumière, demonstrated their camera in the basement of a Paris café. The 30-minute long shows were a great success, and* **cinématographes** *were soon being used around the world.*

French is widely spoken throughout the world. In addition to people in France, tens of millions of people from Belgium, Switzerland, Canada, and countries in Africa, South America, and the Caribbean speak French as their first language. Like Spanish, Italian, Portuguese, and Romanian, French evolved from Latin, a language spoken in Europe 2000 years ago.

Regional languages

A thousand years ago, people in different parts of France spoke different languages. Some of these languages were French dialects, or versions of French. As the French kings, who lived in Paris, became more powerful, they encouraged the use of Parisian French throughout the land. They also established strict rules about correct French spelling, pronunciation, and grammar. Today, nearly everyone uses the same version of French, although a few regional languages, including Provençal in the south, Occitan in the southwest, and Alsatian in the northeast, survive.

The *Académie Française*

Since 1635, the 40 members of the *Académie Française*, or French Academy, have shaped and controlled the French language. These members include political leaders, writers, and scientists. They decide on new words to describe new ideas and inventions. If they feel that too many words are creeping into French from other languages, they replace them with French equivalents. The *Académie* is treated very seriously and with much ceremony. Members, called *Immortels* or "Immortals," hold positions for life and wear traditional costumes that include special hats, swords, and uniforms.

Many English words come from French, especially those that refer to food. Do you recognize any words on this sign which lists the restaurant's specialties?

When the French duke William the Conqueror became King of England in the eleventh century, he made French the language of the English court. That is why so many English words come from French.

Speak in French

Chances are that you already know several French words that are used in everyday English! In fact, just under half of all English words are thought to have come from French. A few include restaurant, cathedral, tourist, menu, dessert, mountain, and chef.

English	French
yes	*oui*
no	*non*
hello	*bonjour*
goodbye	*au revoir*
please	*s'il vous plaît*
thank you	*merci*
excuse me	*excusez-moi*
How are you?	*Comment allez-vous?*
Very well.	*Très bien.*
I don't understand.	*Je ne comprends pas.*

A newsstand sells many different types of magazines.

Reading is a great pastime in France. People always crowd shops and outdoor bookstalls, such as the *bouquinistes* along the Seine River in Paris, looking for interesting reading material. The French are especially proud of their own writers, who have produced some of the most influential and revolutionary literature of the last 300 years.

Novelists

In the 1800s, dramatic stories were very popular. Victor Hugo wrote the classics *Hunchback of Notre Dame* about Quasimodo, a lonely man who lives in the bell towers of Paris's Notre Dame cathedral, and *Les Misérables*, set during the French Revolution. Alexandre Dumas, who created *The Three Musketeers*, was another important writer of this time.

The plays of France's most popular playwright, Jean Baptiste Molière (1622–1673) are still performed in the **Comédie Française,** *a famous theater founded in Paris in 1680.*

In a 1935 film version of **Les Misérables,** *the main character, Jean Valjean, is held by prison guards.*

George Sand (1804–1876) wrote over 100 novels, many of them about the lives of farmers and their families. Born Aurore Dudevant, she, like other female writers of the nineteenth century, changed her name to a man's name to make sure that her work was taken seriously.

Astérix is an ancient warrior who is always saving his village by outsmarting Roman invaders. In the north of France, there is a theme park devoted to the Astérix comic strip.

Sharing ideas

Many of France's writers are known for their important work in philosophy. René Descartes, who lived in the 1600s, is considered the founder of modern philosophy. His famous words, "I think, therefore I am," began a great debate about the human mind. Later philosophers, such as Jean-Jacques Rousseau and Voltaire, criticized the corrupt kings, aristocrats, and priests of their day for treating common people unfairly. Their ideas inspired the overthrow of the **monarchy** during the French Revolution. In the twentieth century, Jean-Paul Sartre, Simone de Beauvoir, and Albert Camus explored the meaning of life in their writing.

Literature for children

French children's literature is enjoyed around the world. One of the best-known stories is Antoine de St-Exupéry's *Le Petit Prince,* or *The Little Prince,* a fable about a traveler from another planet. The fantastic adventures of Babar the elephant, by Jean and Laurent de Brunhoff, and the *Astérix* comic strip, by René Goscinny and Albert Uderzo, are also famous.

For centuries, most French legends and folktales were passed down from generation to generation by storytellers. One of the most popular storytellers was Charles Perrault. Perrault collected and retold tales such as *Sleeping Beauty*, *Little Red Riding Hood*, and *Cinderella* in his famous book *Tales of Mother Goose*.

Some of the oldest French tales are about two storybook knights named Roland and Oliver. This tale tells how the two men became friends during a bitter war.

The Tale of Roland and Oliver

Over a thousand years ago, the mighty **emperor** Charlemagne, who ruled France and Germany, was at war with the powerful Count Girard. For two years, Charlemagne surrounded Girard's castle at the city of Vienne, but could not defeat Girard's soldiers.

One day, Girard's young nephew, Oliver, grew tired of staying in the castle. He put on plain clothes and slipped outside to wander among Charlemagne's soldiers. There, he met the emperor's young nephew, Roland, who was **jousting** with his friends.

Oliver asked to joust and, thinking him an ordinary soldier, the men lent him a horse and **lance**. As Oliver bravely beat them one by one, the other soldiers began to suspect he was one of Count Girard's men and their enemy.

"After him!" Roland shouted, as Oliver galloped away. Roland almost overtook Oliver at the castle entrance, but he let Oliver escape because he admired his bravery.

Afterward, both daring knights thought about one another, wishing that they were not enemies. Oliver pleaded with his uncle to make peace. Count Girard agreed, and sent Oliver to speak with Charlemagne. The emperor refused to end the war, however, so Oliver proposed a plan to Roland, who stood at Charlemagne's side.

"We are well matched in skill," he said. "Shall you and I settle which side wins this war by fighting a duel?" Roland agreed, as did Charlemagne and the Count.

Dressed in armor, the two young knights met in the early morning to battle. They fought for hours, exchanging blows with their swords until their blades were nicked and their armor battered. Then, with a mighty stroke of his sword, Roland shattered Oliver's blade. Oliver thought that Roland would kill him. Instead, the honorable Roland threw aside his sword saying, "I cannot kill an unarmed knight."

They fought with branches and wrestled with their bare hands, but neither could win the duel. At noon, they fell exhausted to the ground.

"I am honored to fight such a worthy knight," said Oliver. "I wish that we were friends and brothers rather than enemies," Roland replied.

Then, a new sword was brought for Oliver, and they fought again. Night came, and still they traded blows in the darkness. Suddenly, the ringing of their swords stopped. The two men had given up their fight. "Neither of us was meant to win this duel," they agreed. "It is a sign that we should make peace — and so should our uncles."

With that, Charlemagne and Count Girard agreed to settle their differences. Roland and Oliver became the best of friends, and never again did they take up arms against one another.

Glossary

abbey A building where monks or nuns live

agricultural Having to do with farming

ancestor A person from whom one is descended

aristocrat A noble or member of the upper class

Aztec Relating to the people who ruled Mexico before the Spanish took it over in the 1600s

beret A soft round cap worn off to one side

capital A city where the government of a state or country is located

cathedral A large church

chapel A room where people pray

civilization A society with a well-established culture that has existed for a long time

composer A person who writes music

controversial Causing a dispute or argument

custom Something that a group of people have done for so long that it becomes an important part of their way of life

denomination An organized religious group

embroider To make a design on cloth using thread

emperor A ruler of a country or group of countries

fable A story that teaches a lesson

fast To stop eating food or certain kinds of food

fortify To strengthen in case of attack, for example by building walls

girder A beam that helps support a building

harvest The gathering of crops

invade To enter using force

joust To battle someone on horseback, using a lance

lance A long wooden pole with a sharp iron or steel head

linen Cloth made from the flax plant

mascot A person, animal, or thing that is believed to bring good luck

military Having to do with the army

monarchy A government that is ruled by a king, queen, emperor, or empress

monk A member of a male religious community who takes certain vows, such as silence or poverty

mural A painting created on a wall or ceiling

nuclear power Energy that is created when atoms come together or split apart

nun A member of a female religious community who lives a life of prayer and service to others, for example, as a teacher or nurse

philosophy The investigation and study of human beliefs and wisdom

priest A religious leader

rebellious Going against the accepted laws and ways of thinking

revolution The overthrow of a government

revolutionary Bringing about great change

tapestry A heavy decorative weaving meant for hanging on walls

temple A building used for religious services

vaccine A preparation of a weakened virus that is given to people so that they can build up their resistance to a stronger form of the virus and not become ill

worship To honor or respect a god

Index

1 2 3 4 5 6 7 8 9 0 Printed in the USA 5 4 3 2 1 0